EYE TO EYE WITH DOGS

LABRADOR RETRIEVERS

Lynn M. Stone

Rourke

Publishing LLC
Vero Beach, Florida 32964

www.rourkepublishing.com

PHOTO CREDITS: All photos © Lynn M. Stone

Cover: *The first Labrador retrievers came from Newfoundland in northeastern Canada in the early 1800s.*

Acknowledgments: For their help in the preparation of this book, the author thanks humans Missy Brown, June Connelly, Chris Cornelius of Marsh Mutt Manor Labradors (Warsaw, IN), Jennifer Lee, and Alice Monroe; and canines Cuda, Daisy, McKenzie, Molly, Tally, Teke, and others.

Editor: Frank Sloan

Cover and page design by Nicola Stratford

Library of Congress Cataloging-in-Publication Data

Stone, Lynn M.
    Labrador retrievers / Lynn M. Stone
        p. cm. — (Eye to eye with dogs)
    Summary: A brief introduction to the physical characteristics, temperament, uses, and breeding history of the labrador retriever.
    Includes bibliographical references (p.).
    ISBN 1-58952-329-6
    1. Labrador retriever—Juvenile literature. [1. Labrador retriever. 2. Dogs.] I. Title.

SF429.L3 S76 2002
636.752'7—dc21   2002017838

Printed in the USA

MP/W

Table of Contents

The Labrador Retriever   5

Labs at Work   7

Labradors of the Past   11

Looks   17

Labrador Companions   18

A Note About Dogs   22

Glossary   23

Index   24

Further Reading/Websites   24

Popular Labrador retrievers have warm, winning personalities.

The Labrador Retriever

Labrador retrievers are big, gentle dogs with great **instincts** to retrieve. Retrieving dogs are especially good at being trained to bring objects back to their owners.

LABRADOR RETRIEVER FACTS

Weight: 55-80 pounds (25-36 kilograms)
Height: 21.5-24.5 inches (55-62 centimeters)
Country of Origin: Canada
Life Span: 12-13 years

Labrador retrievers are easily the most popular **purebred** dogs in both the United States and Canada. American Kennel Club (AKC) records show that Labs took the number one position in 1991. They continue to hold it into the new century.

A Lab plunges into wintry water to retrieve a mallard duck for its master.

Labs at Work

Labs are one of just three dog **breeds** commonly used as guide, or seeing-eye, dogs. These dogs undergo almost two years of training at special schools. Then they can begin work with their blind masters. Some Labs are trained to work with people who have other **disabilities**.

A trusty, highly trained yellow Lab stands with its blind master.

Labs are also used as search and rescue dogs. Some worked at the World Trade Center disaster in New York City in 2001. Labs are most popular, though, as family companions.

Labs are one breed in the group of sporting, or gun, dogs. Hunters use hard-working Labs to retrieve many kinds of game birds, especially ducks and geese.

Mallard in mouth, a hard-working Lab returns to its master.

Modern Labs are true water dogs, like their ancestors.

Labradors of the Past

Labrador is a large territory in eastern Canada. One can certainly find Labrador retrievers there. But the first Labs were from Newfoundland. Newfoundland is a province in cold, foggy northeastern Canada.

With their dense, black coats, the first Lab-like retrievers were true water dogs. They retrieved ducks, geese, and even fish. They also pulled small fishing boats in icy water.

These black Lab pups will grow up to love water.

Retrieving objects comes naturally to Labradors.

These dogs of the early 1800s were called St. John's Newfoundland dogs. St. John's is the largest city in Newfoundland. Curiously, dogs of this type began to die out. One reason was a costly dog tax in Newfoundland.

Many of the St. John's Newfoundlands, however, had been taken to England in the early 1800s. English dog **breeders mated** some of their Newfoundlands with other retrievers. Over many years, the result of their work was the modern, water-loving Labrador retriever.

Hanging out in a marsh is something Labradors love to do.

A female Lab shows the warm personality and kindly expression of her breed.

Looks

Labs have short, straight coats over dense undercoats. The undercoat keeps them warm in most weather conditions.

The early Labs were black. In more recent years, breeders have developed "yellow" and "chocolate" Labs, too.

Labs have broad heads with floppy ears and strong, fairly square jaws. Their tails are long and straight, and rounded like a flagpole.

Labrador Companions

Good Labs are wonderful companions for children or adults. They are quick to learn, **obedient**, good-natured, and trusting. They are comfortable with strangers and other pets.

Yellow Lab pups grow up to be great canine companions.

A yellow Lab plants a wet whisper by her master's ear.

Indoors, Labs are usually calm and not quick to bark unless startled. Outdoors, Labs love to run, swim, and, of course, retrieve.

Labs do very well in obedience trials. Obedience trials test how well a dog has learned to follow human commands. In field obedience trials, Labs show their skills at retrieving birds or following a scent.

Some Lab owners enter their dogs in **conformation** shows. Conformation shows judge how well a dog meets the ideal shape and structure of its breed.

This Lab is a champion in field obedience.

A Note About Dogs

Puppies are cute and cuddly, but buying one should never be done without serious thought. Choosing the right breed of dog requires some homework. And remember that a dog will require more than love and great patience. It will require food, exercise, grooming, a warm, safe place to live, and medical care.

A dog can be your best friend, but you need to be its best friend, too. For more information about buying and owning a dog, contact the American Kennel Club at http://www.akc.org/index.cfm or the Canadian Kennel Club at http:// www.ckc.ca/.

Glossary

breeders (BREE duhrz) — people who raise animals, such as dogs, and carefully choose the mothers and fathers for more dogs

breeds (BREEDZ) — particular kinds of domestic animals within a larger group, such as the Labrador retriever breed within the dog group

conformation (con fohr MAYshun) — the desired form and structure of an animal based on its breed

disabilities (dis eh BIL eh teez) — losses of abilities, such as deafness being the loss of hearing ability

instincts (IN stinktz) — actions or behaviors with which an animal is born, rather than learned behaviors

mated (MAY tud) — to have been paired with another dog for the purpose of having pups

obedient (oh BEE dee ent) — showing the ability to follow directioms or commands

purebred (PYOOR bred) — an animal of a single (pure) breed

Index

American Kennel Club 6

breeders 14

breeds 7

coats 12, 17

guide dogs 7

instincts 5

Labrador 11

Newfoundland 11

obedience trials 20

retrievers 12, 14

St. John's Newfoundland
dogs 13, 14

search and rescue dogs 8

Further Reading

Wilcox, Charlotte: *The Labrador Retriever.* Capstone Press, 1996

Websites to Visit

Labrador Retriever Home Page at http://www.labradorhome.com/
Labrador Retrievers at http://www.k9web.com/dog-
faqs/breeds/labradors.html
Working Retriever Central at http://www.working-retriever.com/

About the Author

Lynn Stone is the author of over 400 children's books. He is a talented
natural history photographer as well. Lynn, a former teacher, travels
worldwide to photograph wildlife in its natural habitat.